The Supreme
Solution to the so-called NEGROES' Problem

by

Mr. Elijah Muhammad

Messenger of Allah

to the Lost-Found Nation of Islam in North America

ᴥᴥ ᴥᴥ ᴥᴥ ᴥᴥ ᴥᴥ ᴥᴥ ᴥᴥ ᴥᴥ ᴥᴥ ᴥᴥ ᴥᴥ ᴥᴥ ᴥᴥ ᴥᴥ ᴥᴥ ᴥᴥ

"Islam Means Freedom,

Justice and Equality"

-- Mr. Elijah Muhammad

ᴥᴥ ᴥᴥ ᴥᴥ ᴥᴥ ᴥᴥ ᴥᴥ ᴥᴥ ᴥᴥ ᴥᴥ ᴥᴥ ᴥᴥ ᴥᴥ ᴥᴥ ᴥᴥ ᴥᴥ ᴥᴥ

Published By
**Messenger Elijah Muhammad Propagation Society
(M.E.M.P.S.)**
P.O. Box 162412 • Atlanta, GA 30321
(770) 907-2212 For Catalog

First Edition

February 26, 1957

Under the title "Mr. Muhammad Speaks", writings and teachings of Mr. Elijah Muhammad are printed weekly in the "Pittsburgh Courier", which claims to have a circulation of almost 200,000.

Printed in U. S. A.

بسم الله الرحمن الرحيم
نحمده ونصلي ونسلم على رسوله سيدنا محمد خاتم النبيين

Introduction

By Mr. Abdul Basit Naeem, Editor-Publisher, MOSLEM WORLD & THE U.S.A.

It is with pleasure that I am writing these few lines of Introduction of Mr. Elijah Muhammad, the author of this book.

Mr. Elijah Muhammad is the leader and spiritual head of several thousand Moslems in the United States of America, all of whom are of African descent and converts from Christianity.

While Mr. Elijah Muhammad's Moslem movement has no special name, its members are generally known as "The Temple of Islam" people, for that is what their house of worship and instruction is called: "The Temple of Islam." There are at present over twenty such temples in the U. S. A. — in the states of New York, Michigan, Illinois, New Jersey, Connecticut, Massachusetts, Pennsylvania, Wisconsin, Georgia and Ohio and in the District of Columbia.

Mr. Elijah Muhammad's movement is also known for its highly successful and smart business enterprises around the country, which include farms, apartment houses, restaurants, grocery stores and bakeries. A number of Mr. Elijah Muhammad's followers own and operate a variety of businesses, such as barber and shoe repair shops and dry cleaning plants.

In Mr. Elijah Muhammad's words, and as confirmed by many U. S. Moslem authorities, the Moslem movement of which he is the head is "the fastest growing Moslem religious body in North America." Dozens of men and women are said to join its ranks each month.

Mr. Elijah Muhammad is the only Moslem leader in this country I know of who is actively engaged, through his writings (he writes a column each week in the "Pittsburgh Courier," which has a national circulation of nearly 200,000 copies per issue) and Temples of Islam and its members, in seeking converts to Islam. Others, at least so it seems to me, are only interested in "defending" Islam or preaching "Moslem-Christian brotherhood." In the opinion of Mr. Elijah Muhammad, "this is no time to think of anyone other than our own, especially when the Holy Quran itself, in Chapter 5:54, speaks against friendship with Christians as well as Jews."

Mr. Elijah Muhammad, again, is the only Moslem leader in this country who has paid some attention to the educational problems of his people. (My friends might dispute this statement and say that *I* have done more in this respect. However, I cannot consider such an impression on the part of my friends to be entirely correct. I am, after all, only a writer and publisher, and not a leader of any Moslem group or movement.) The University of Islam in Chicago, which Mr. Elijah Muhammad founded a few years ago, and which now has more than two hundred students on its rolls, is an outstanding example of his accomplishments in this direction and an everlasting tribute to his leadership.

I am, of course, fully aware of the fact that some of the teachings of Mr. Elijah Muhammad, which have been included in this book, would not be acceptable to Moslems in the East without, perhaps, some sort of an explanation by the author or by someone who can interpret them well. The Moslem leader himself knows this, and he is perfectly frank about it. As he told me a few months ago, "My brothers in the East were never subjected to conditions of slavery and systematic brainwashing by the slavemasters for as long a period of time as my people here were subjected. I cannot, therefore, blame them if they differ with me in certain interpretations of the Message of Islam. In fact, I do not even *expect* them to understand some of the things I say unto my people here."

As far as I am concerned, I consider the differences between Islam of the East and teachings of Mr. Elijah Muhammad to be of relatively minor importance *at this time*, because these are not related to the *SPIRIT* of Islam, which, I am sure, is completely shared by *all* of us. A Moslem from Pakistan, Indonesia, Iran or Egypt only has to meet some of Mr. Elijah Muhammad's follow-

ers to be convinced of their love, utmost devotion and passion for all that is the *true* Islamic Spirit.

Not many of Mr. Elijah Muhammad's followers have had the opportunity to read and understand the Holy Quran or fully comprehend the concept of Moslem prayers, fasting, *zakat* (alms-giving) and the institution of *hadj* (pilgrimage to Mecca). However, I am in a position to say, most authoritatively, that Moslems under the leadership of Mr. Muhammad have now BEGUN to make a serious study of Allah's Divine Word and to grasp its true meaning. Very soon, I can further state, they will also start receiving instruction in the daily prayers and other Islamic duties.

I know of what I have just said, in the preceding paragraph, because I am the humble individual through whom Mr. Elijah Muhammad's followers are obtaining their copies of the Holy Quran and other Islamic literature, and I know that they have already acquired more copies of the Holy Quran than might be in the possession of *all* the other Moslems in the U. S. A.!

The Spirit of Islam which prevails in the heart of each of Mr. Elijah Muhammad's followers can also be judged by the attention that he (or she) pays to such important aspects of life as food and clothing. A follower of Mr. Elijah Muhammad will never eat outside of his home, except in a Moslem-owned restaurant. Members of the Temples of Islam never touch pork, ham bacon, lard "or any other filth" — forbidden by Allah. They do not take intoxicants of any type, and they do not even smoke. And most of them are known to eat but one meal a day!

As for clothing, men and women who are members of the Temples of Islam in the United States, wear only Moslem-style garb. The women are especially careful in the selection of their clothes. They do not permit themselves to be attracted by "the latest trends in fashion, which can only suit the beasts."

The followers of Islam under the guidance of Mr. Elijah Muhammad do not go dancing, dating or nightclubbing. Nor do they participate in or attend any other function or activity that is "unlawful in the eyes of Allah and Islam."

Small wonder, then, that some of the Eastern Moslems in America who do not faithfully observe the Divine restrictions do not appreciate Mr. Elijah Muhammad's mission and achievements.

Despite Mr. Elijah Muhammad's "blunt techniques" and a few controversial teachings about certain aspects of Islam, I have nothing but the utmost respect for the Moslem leader. I do indeed appreciate his efforts to bring the black people of America "back into the fold of Islam," which, in his opinion,

as in mine, is the only solution to their basic problems. Islam alone, undoubtedly, will elevate the status of those among the so-called "Negroes" in America who are down-trodden and in a pitiable mental condition. I believe that the so-called "Negroes" need Allah and His Religion of Peace, Justice and Equality —Islam. Islam can and *will* give them a New Life and assurance of seeing the Hereafter.

Americans of African descent, I believe, should be grateful that the Message of Allah has, at last, been brought to them, through the person of the author of this book, Mr. Elijah Muhammad.

—*Abdul Basit Naeem*
Servant of Islam; Editor-Publisher,
MOSLEM WORLD & THE U.S.A.

475-A First Street
Brooklyn 15, N. Y.

Preface

By Mr. Malcolm X., Minister, Muhammad's Temple of Islam No. 7

If TRANSFORMATION is the yardstick by which the strength of religious Truth should be measured, let us examine and see what sort of change the Message of the Honorable ELIJAH MUHAMMAD has brought about in his followers during the short while he has been teaching here in America...and thereby judge hime according to the RESULTS of his teachings among us.

Before hearing his soul-stirring Message, the religion that our Slavemaster had brainwashed us with was one in which we served many idols and stayed bewildered and upset by a conglomeration of confusing doctrines. The Slavemaster called our church the "NEGRO CHURCH", to let the world know that "ours" was a church seperate, distinct and apart from his own Christian Church which he had every intention of keeping Lily White. In fact, the Negro Church was just a futile attempt to imitate the white church of the Slavemaster...even going so far as to parrot the Slavemaster's lying doctrine that all black people were cursed by God to work for the white Christians. Our churches stayed torn apart by argument and jealousies of petty leaders who wanted power for themselves, and were therefore constantly creating "new denominations" and setting up factions of their own, that kept us confused and divided against each other. In fact, strangely enough, the unity of the Negro Churches (IN THE PAST) never constituted a threat to the Slavemaster, but was a constant source of disunity AMONG US, and AGAINST US.

Furthermore, before receiving the Light of Islam from the Teachings of Messenger Muhammad, most of us were an illiterate and ignorant people who not only despised education and intelligence, but were even suspicious and wary of those of our own kind who had it. We had no knowledge of anything other than what the Slavemaster taught us, and took everything he said just as though it was the gospel truth, without examining it and looking into it for ourselves, just because "HE" (the white Christian) said it. We knew nothing of our own glorious history, our religion, and our own God. We even accepted all of the stereotyped doctrines the Slavemaster taught us about ourselves, no matter how degrading it was. We didn't think our Christian Slavemaster would purposely lie. In fact, many of us thought that white Christians could do no wrong and could speak no wrong. No wonder we were divided. No wonder we hated ourselves. We hated what we had been taught we were. We fought among ourselves at the slightest provocation, filling the hospitals and the cemeteries with our own kind, ... and at the very same time our own religious leaders were teaching us to love, be patient, understanding, forgiving (turn-the-other-cheek) TO THE CRUEL SLAVEMASTER. We were kind to OUR ENEMY, but viciously impatient and cruel toward ourselves.

As "Negro Christians" we idolized our Christian Slavemaster, and lived for the day when his plurality (trinity) of white gods would allow us to mingle and mix up with them. We worshipped the false beauty of the Slavemaster's leprous looking women. Our greatest desire was to have one of them even if it meant death. We regarded them with the utmost respect, courtesy and kindness, bowing and tipping our hats, showing our teeth. We perfected the art of

Mr. Malcolm X.

humility and politness for their sake. . . but at the same time we treated our own women as if they were mere animals, with no love, respect or protection, beating and abusing them even in public places, selling them from man to man, letting all other races (even the Slavemaster) mix freely with them, having no regard whatsoever for their feelings, in public or in private.

No one had more "Christian Churches" than we, yet our morals were at their lowest. Bastard babies of all shades were in abundance, often carrying the mark of the Slavemaster's adulterous blood (mail men, milk men, insurance men, and other bill collectors).

We were supposed to be a part of the "Christian Church" yet we lived in a bitter world of dejection, caused by our being rejected by the white Christian Church". In large numbers we became victims of drunkenness, drug addiction, reefer smoking, . . . in a false and futile

attempt to "escape" the reality and horrors of the shameful condition that the Slavemaster's Christian religion had placed us in.

Loathsome diseases caused by too close a contact with the weak-blooded white race ran rampant through us.

Our economic plight was so pitiful, and our hope of sufficient FOOD, CLOTH-ING, and SHELTER was so remote that we turned to vices of the very lowest sort, to gambling and games of chance, hoping that just one "lucky number" would put us in reach of the necessities of life again for ourselves and our families. Yes, many of us who were even the "pillars of the church" were artful thieves, master liars and often the organizers of the very evils that were tearing our people apart.

Fear ruled us, but not fear of God. We had fear of the Slavemaster, we had no knowledge of Truth and we were apparently afraid to let him see us advocating or practicing love and unity towards each other. We were not man enough to stand up and protect our own kind from the lyncher's rope or from the Slavemaster's acts of rape, but at the same time we would go around the world fighting others in behalf and in defense of our Slavemaster.

Is it a wonder that the world laughed at us, ridiculed us and held us to scorn? We practiced love of others, while hating ourselves. . .patience with others and impatience with our own kind. . .unity with others and disunity with our own kind. We called ourselves "Negro Christians", yet we remained an ignorant, foolish people, despised and REJECTED ' by the white Christians. We were fools!

ALL PRAISE IS DUE TO ALLAH, Creator of Heaven and Earth. Just as surely as Seasons bring about changes in the Earth, today TIME is bringing about a CHANGE in our condition. An earth-shaking REFORMATION is taking place among the so-called Negroes in America. Almighty God ALLAH has appeared in our midst and raised from among us a REFORMER in the person of the Honorable ELIJAH MUHAMMAD, the MESSENGER with a Message for us. His work among us has already produced results unequaled in history.

His Message shows us how the "Christianity" offered us by the Slavemaster has failed to give us Freedom, Justice, and Equality ... How we yet are not treated as citizens in the governments of Christianity ... How it has neither enlightened nor elevated us. It has not succeeded in uniting us with love and Brotherhood.

The soul-stirring, life-giving Message of the Honorable ELIJAH MUHAMMAD is bringing us together today, and uniting us into a vast Brotherhood under ONE GOD ALLAH overnight. He has filled us with an unquenchable thirst for education, knowledge and wisdom. He has given us the desire not only to know ALLAH now, but to be with Him in the hereafter. His Message of Truth has cured us of Drunkenness and dope addiction and other vices that were destroying our morals. He is teaching us the importance of respecting and protecting our women, and placing them on the highest pinnacle of civilization, giving them castles and treating them like Queen Mothers of civilization that they are. Among those of us who follow him adultery and fornication has completely disappeared. Lying and stealing has been stamped out.

No more are we filled with fear of the Slavemaster. We now have ONE GOD, ONE RELIGION, ONE LEADER and TEACHER, this ONENESS gives us a UNITY never before attained by any other people (in such a short period of time) in history.

On the following pages of this Book are portions of the MESSAGE being taught us by the Honorable ELIJAH MUHAMMAD. May Almighty ALLAH open your heart that you too may receive understanding and LIGHT from His Words...and become guided by His Light forever-more.

CONTENTS

9

The word "Allah" written in Arabic, the language of the Holy Quran.

The Coming of Allah

"Allah came to us from the Holy City of Mecca, Arabia, in 1930.

"He used the name of Wallace D. Fard, often signing it W. D. Fard. In the third year (1933) He signed His name 'W. F. Muhammad' which stands for Wallace Fard Muhammad.

"He came alone.

Allah Forgives

"Regardless of our sins that we have committed in following and obeying our slavemasters, Allah will forgive us if we (the so-called Negroes) turn to Him and return to our own kind."

What Allah Taught Us

"Allah taught us the Knowledge of ourselves, of Himself (God) and the devil, the Measurement of the Earth, other Planets and the Civilizations of some of the Planets other than Earth.

"He measured and weighed the Earth and its water, (and taught us of these,) and the history of the Moon, and the history of the two nations that dominate the earth, black and white.

"He gave us information as to the exact birth of the white race and the name of their God who made them, and how, and the end of their time. Also, the Judgement, how it would begin and end.

"He taught us the truth of how we were made slaves, and how we are kept in slavery by the slave-masters' children.

"Allah declared the doom of America, for her evils to us it was past due. and that she is number one to be destroyed, but her judgement could not take place until we (the so-called Negroes) hear the truth.

"He declared that we were without the knowledge of self or anyone else, and had been made blind, deaf and dumb by this white race of people, and that we must return to our people, our God (Allah) and His Religion of Peace (Islam)—the Religion of the Prophets.

Allah's Warning To Us

"Allah told us that the slavemasters had taught us to eat the wrong food, and that this wrong food was the cause of our sickness and short span of life. He declared that He would heal us, and sit us in Heaven at once if we would submit to Him; otherwise He would chastise us with a severe chastisement until we did submit, and that He was able to force the whole world into submission to His will."

Allah's Promise To Us

"Allah said that He would make a new people out of us who submit to Him by causing us to grow into a new growth, not an entirely new body but a reversal of the old decayed body into a new growth, which, He said, would make us all as we were at the age of 16. And there will be no decay in this new growth of life. He also stated that the next life is that of unlimited progress."

Be Yourself

BE YOURSELF

"Allah's greatest teaching and warning to us (the so-called Negroes) is: *Be Yourself!*

The Bible and It's Teachings

" I do not know of any scriptural book or religion that does not contain some good. What Allah demands today is a book or religion that is *all* good, not a mixture of truth and falsehood, not a book or religion that is or has been tampered with by His enemies.

"The Bible is called a Holy Book, and is often referred to as the Word of God. The present English edition is said to be translated out of the original tongues into the present English language by the authority of one King James in 1611.

"What is the original tongue or language that the Bible was written in? What language did Moses speak? Originally, the Torah (Old Testament) was given to Musa (Moses) in 2000 B. C., who spoke ancient Egyptian Arabic, and the second half (New Testament) was revealed to Isa (Jesus) 2000 years ago, and he (Jesus) spoke both Arabic and Hebrew.

"From the first day that the white race received the Divine Scripture they started tampering with its truth to make it to suit themselves and blind the black man. It is their nature to do evil and the book cannot be recognized as the pure and Holy Word of God.

"The Bible is now being called the *poison book* by God Himself, and who can deny that it is not poison?

"It has poisoned the very hearts and minds of the so-called Negroes so much that they can't agree with each other.

"The Bible opens with the words of someone other than God trying to represent God and His creation to us. This is called the Book of Moses and reads as following: 'In the beginning God created the Heaven and the earth.' (Gen. 1:1) When was this beginning? There in the Genesis the writer tells us that it was 4,004 B. C. This we know, now, that it refers to the making of the white race, and not the Heaven and the earth.

"The second verse of the First Chapter of Genesis reads: 'And the earth was without form and void; darkness was upon the deep and the spirit of God moved upon the face of the waters.' What was the water on, since there was no form of earth? As I see it, the Bible is very questionable.

"After God had created everything

without asking for any help from anyone, then comes His weakness in the 26th verse of the same chapter (Genesis). He invites us to help Him make a man. Allah has revealed that it was *us* that was invited to make a man (white race). A man is far more easy to make than the Heaven and the earth. We can't charge these questionable readings of the Bible to Moses because he was a Prophet of God and they (Prophets) don't lie.

"If the present Bible is the direct Word of God, why isn't God speaking rather than His Prophet Musa? Neither does Moses tell us here in the first chapter of Genesis that it is from God. No, we don't find the name Moses mentioned in the chapter.

"The Bible is the graveyard of my poor people (the so-called Negroes) and I would like to dwell upon it until I am sure that they understand that it is not quite as holy as they first thought it was.

"I don't mean to say that there is no truth in it. Certainly, plenty of truth, *if understood.*

"Will you (the so-called Negroes) accept the understanding of it?

"The Bible charges all of its great Prophets with evil, it makes God guilty of an act of adultery by charging Him with being the father of Mary's baby (Jesus); again it charges Noah and Lot with drunkenness and Lot getting children by his daughter.

"What a poison book!

"We, being robbed so thoroughly of the Knowledge of self and kind, are opposed to our own salvation in favor of our enemies, and I here quote another poison addition of the slavery teaching of the Bible: 'Love your enemies, bless them who curse you, pray for those who spitefully use you, him that smiteth thee on one cheek offer the other cheek, him that taketh (robs) away the cloak, forbid not to take (away) thy coat also.' (Luke 6:27-29)

"The slavemasters couldn't have found a better teaching for their protection against the slaves' possible dissatisfaction of their masters' brutal treatment."

Cause for The Nation of Islam to Rejoice

"If a man can rejoice over the finding of his lost or strayed animal, or a piece of silver, or a son who had the desire to leave his home to practice the evil habits of strangers, how much more should Allah and the Nation of Islam rejoice over finding *us* who have been lost from (Allah and the Nation of Islam) for 400 years and following others than our own kind?"

Christianity

"Christianity is a religion organized and backed by the devils for the purpose of making slaves of black mankind.

"Freedom, Justice, Equality; money, good homes, etc.—these Christianity cannot give us (not the Christianity that has been taught us).

"He (Allah) said that Christianity was

organized by the white race and they placed the name of Jesus on it being the founder and author to deceive black people into accepting it.

"Our first step is to give back to the white man his religion, Christianity, church and his names. These three are chains of slavery that hold us in bondage to them. We are free only when we give up the above three.

"The Bible, church and Christianity have deceived the so-called Negroes. I pray (to) Allah to giv them life, and light of understanding."

Preacher of Christianity

"The greatest hindrance to the truth of our people is the preacher of Christianity. He won't accept it, nor is he content to let others alone who are trying to accept it. He is the man who stands in the way of the salvation of his people and as soon as people awaken to the knowledge of this man in their way to God, freedom, justice and equality and stop following him, the sooner they will be in heaven while they live. The preachers are afraid of the truth."

Christians

"The followers of Isa (Jesus) and the *Injeel* (Bible) or gospel revealed to him are referred to as Christians.

"They believe that both Musa and Isa were Jews."

Destruction of the World

"Allah has warned us of how He would (one day) destroy the world with bombs, poison gas, and finally fire that would consume and destroy everything of the present world. Not anything of it (the present world of white mankind) would be left. Those escaping the destruction would not be allowed to take anything of it out with them.

"Allah (has) pointed out to us a dreadful looking plane that is made like a wheel in the sky today. It is a half-mile by a half-mile square; it is a human-built planet. (I won't go into all of the details here, but it is up there and can be seen twice a week; it is no secret.) Ezekiel saw it a long time ago. It was built for the purpose of destroying the present world. Allah has also hinted at plaguing the world with rain, snow, hail and earthquakes."

There Can Be No Love for an Enemy

"It is against the very nature of God, and man, and all life, to love their enemies. Would God ask us to do that which He Himself cannot do? He hates His enemies so much that He tells us that He is going to destroy them in hellfire, along with those of us who follow His enemies."

What Our Enemy Is Doing

"The enemy is alert, wide-awake and

ever on the job to prevent the so-called Negroes from believing in Allah and the True Religion of Allah and His Prophets —the Religion of Islam. The enemy is well-aware that Allah is the Rock of our Defense and Islam is the House of our Salvation.

Mr. Fard Muhammad

"Mr. Fard Muhammad (God in Person) chose to suffer three and one-half years to show his love for his people who have suffered over 300 years at the hands of a people who by nature are evil, wicked, and have no good in them.

"He was persecuted, sent to jail in 1932, and ordered out of Detroit, Michigan, May 26, 1933. He came to Chicago in the same year, arrested almost immediately on his arrival and placed behind prison bars.

"He submitted himself with all humbleness to his persecutors. Each time he was arrested, he sent for me that I may see and learn the price of TRUTH for us (the so-called Negroes).

"He was able to save himself from such suffering, but how else was the scripture to be fulfilled? We followed in his footsteps suffering the same persecution."

Fear

"Fear is the worst enemy that we (the so-called Negroes) have, but entire submission to Allah and His Messenger will remove this fear. The white race put fear in our foreparents when they were babies, so says the Word of Allah.

"The poor (so-called) Negroes are so filled with fear of their enemy that they stoop to helping him against their own salvation.

"Be aware of what you are doing lest you be the worse loser. If they had only been taught the TRUTH, they would act differently."

John Hawkins

"Allah has taught us that our foreparents were deceived and brought into America by a slave-trader whose name was John Hawkins in the year 1555."

Heaven on Earth

"He (Allah) has made it clear what constitutes heaven on earth: Freedom, Justice, Equality; money, good homes and friendship in all walks of life.

The Future Holy Book

"The Holy Quran, the Glorious Book, should be read and studied by us (the so-called Negroes). Both the present Bible and the Holy Quran must soon give way to that holy book which no man as yet but Allah has seen. The teachings (prophecies) of the present Bible and the Quran take us up to the resurrection and judgement of this world but not into the next life. That which is in that holy book is for the righteous and their future only; not for the mixed world of righteous and evil.

"The preparation for that unseen life is now going on in the few believers of Islam in Amrica. Islam is the true religion of Allah and it makes a distinction between the lovers of righteousness and lovers of evil. It is that which Allah is using today to separate the righteous from the evil-doers."

No "Integration"

"The slavemasters' children are doing everything in their power to prevent the so-called Negroes from accepting their own God and salvation, by putting on a great show of false love and friendship.

"This is being done through 'integrtion' as it is called, that is, so-called Negroes and whites mixing together, such as in schools, churches, and even intermarriage with the so-called Negroes, and this the poor slaves really think that they are entering a condition of heaven with their former slave-holders, but it will prove to be their doom.

"Today, according to God's word, we are living in a time of great separation between the blacks and whites.

"The prophesized 400 years of slavery —that we the so-called Negroes would have to serve (the white) people—ended in 1955. The so-called Negroes must now return to their own; nothing else will solve their problem.

"The divine power is working and will continue to work in favor of the so-called Negroes' return to their own. The separation would be a blessing for both sides.

Islam

"Allah (Himself) chose for us ISLAM as a religion.

"ISLAM is our salvation. It removes fear, grief and sorrow from any believer and it brings to us peace of mind and contentment.

Jesus of the Bible

"The so-called Negroes must get away from the old slavery teaching that Jesus, who died two thousand years ago, is still alive somewhere waiting and listening to their prayers.

"He (Jesus) was only a prophet like Moses and the other prophets and had the same religion (Islam). He did his work and is dead like others of his time, and has no knowledge of their prayers to him.

"Since Islam over-ran mankind in the 7th Century after Jesus and is still a power of man, why didn't the translators of the Bible mention it? Why didn't they give us the names of the religions of the prophets since they claim a religion for Jesus?

"The history of this man Jesus has been greatly misunderstood by us, the so-called Negroes.

"Jesus" The Ship

"John Hawkins brought our forefathers here (from Africa) on a ship named 'Jesus'; when this ship when on its way back from another load of our people, our foreparents stared at the old slave ship as it departed and begged to be carried back, but to no avail, and they said that 'you can have this new Western world but give us the ship Jesus back to our people and country,' which now has become a song among our people, which goes something like this: 'You-can - have - all - the - world - but - give - me - Jesus.'

"But our foreparents did not know at that time it would be 400 years from that day before the real ship (God Himself) would come and get them and their children and cut loose every link of the slave chain that holds us in bondage to our slave-masters by giving us a true knowledge of self, God and the devil and wipe away the 400 years of tears, weeping, mourning and groaning under the yoke of bondage to the merciless murderers.

Jews, or Hebrews

"Believers in Musa (Moses) and the Torah are referred to as Jews or Hebrews.

"The Jews or Hebrews believe that Musa (Moses) was a Jew, who brought them the Torah.

Judgement of the World

"The judgement of the world has arrived and the gathering together of the people is now going on.

"Why should there be a judgement of the world? Why was there a judgement of the people of Noah and Lot? The Bible says: 'That day shall not come except there come a falling away first, and the man of sin revealed, the son of Perdition' (II Thessalonians 2:3).

"The whole world of our kind awaits the awakening (to the knowledge of the good that is being carried on for their deliverance), and (our awakening) is the last step in the Resurrection and judgement of the world.

"The end of the world has arrived and most of us knoow it, and our enemy's greatest desire is that we remain asleep.

Lazarus

"We have made the grave mistake of Lazarus and the Prodigal Son (St. Luke, Chapter 15), the one who was so charmed over the wealth and food of the rich man that he couldn't leave his gate to seek same for himself. Regardless to the disgraceful condition in which the rich man put him, even to sending his dogs to attack him. The angels then had to come and take him away.

The Lost-Found Nation

"Allah greatly rejoiced over us and was real happy that He had found us— the lost Nation of Islam in the wilderness of North America.

Man of Sin

"The man of sin referred to in the Bible (II Thessalonians 2:3) is now being revealed. He is the devil in person, who was made of sin, not any good was in the essence that he was from. Since he was made of sin, what good can one expect of the man of sin?

"Why has he (the man of sin) been hidden from the eyes of the righteous people and only revealed today? The answer is: How could the man of sin rule the righteous for six thousand years if he had not been veiled to prevent the discovery of his true self?

"According to II Thessalonians 2:9, the man of sin had a work to do and God wouldn't interfere with this work of the man of sin until the time given him was fully up.

"The eighth verse in II Thessalonians reads that the Lord shall consume with the Spirit (of Truth of the man of sin) of his mouth, and shall destroy with the Brightness of His Coming, which means that the truth of the man of sin is clearly made by God that there can be no doubt that he is really the man of sin who has caused and is causing all the trouble among the righteous. He (the man of sin) is a great deceiver, liar and a murderer by nature.

Muhammad the Prophet

"Muhammad, an Arab, was a member of the black nation.

"The Jews and Christians are of the white race, and they don't believe in Muhammad as a prophet of God. Naturally they don't believe in the Scripture (of Muhammad) — The Holy Quran— that Allah revealed to him.

"The Arabs or Muslims have tried and are still trying to get the white race to believe and recognize Muhammad as a Divine Prophet of Allah, and the Quran, a Divine Revelation, as they recognize Musa (Moses) and Isa (Jesus) and the Bible coming from Allah (God).

Muslims

"Believers in ALL of the Prophets of God and the Scriptures—Torah, Bible, Quran—are referred to as Muslims.

"The Muslims make (recognize) no difference in any of the Scriptures as long as these are from Allah.

"They (Muslims) believe in Moses and Jesus, also the true Scriptures that these two prophets brought to their people.

Muslim Prayer Service

"The Muslim Prayer service and its meaning is so beautiful that I am having it put into a small book for my people who believe.

The So-Called Negroes Lack Knowledge of Self

"All nations know and love their members, but the so-called Negroes are (even) afraid to act too friendly towards each other. They are educated in everything but the love and knowledge of self: therefore they will never enjoy love and unity until they are taught the knowledge of self and kind.

"The so-called Negroes must know the

Truth, but surely they will (reject) and are rejecting it.

"The so-called Negroes are absolutely friendless and have sought in vain friendship from their enemies, due to the ignorance of self and their enemies.

"Seek FIRST the friendship of your own people and then the friendship of others (if there is any friendship in others).

The So-Called Negroes Must Work

"Many of us, the so-called Negroes, today are so lazy that we are willing to suffer anything rather than go to work.

"It is true that God has come to sit us in heaven, but not a heaven wherein we won't have to work.

"We must have for our peace and happiness that which other nations have.

"Allah desires to make the black nation the equal or superior of the white race.

The So-Called Negroes Mentioned in New Testament

"We the so-called Negroes are mentioned in the New Testament under several names and parables.

"I will name two: the parable of the Lost Sheep and of the Prodigal Son (Luke 15:1-11), of which we could not be described better under or in a parable.

"Before the coming of Allah (God) we, being blind, deaf and dumb, had mistaken the true meanings of these parables to be referring to the Jews. Now, thanks to Almighty Allah, who came in the Person of Master Fard Muhammad (to whom be praised forever), who has opened my blinded eyes, loosened the knot in my tongue, and has made us to understand that these Bible parables are referring to us, the so-called Negroes (and our slavemasters).

"The answer (Luke 15:4-6) to the charges made by the proud and unholy Pharisees against Him (God in Person) for eating' with His lost-found people whom the Pharisees and their people had made sinners can't be better. It defends Him and His people (lost and found sheep). He proved their wickedness and hatred for His love for His people who were lost and He had found them. They (the Pharisees) had more love for a lost and found animal of theirs than they did for the lost and found people of Allah (God).

Original People

"Allah has taught us that we the so-called Negroes are the original people of the earth who have no birth record.

Pharaoh

"Remember the disgrace suffered by Pharaoh and his people for their opposition against Moses and his followers, just because Pharaoh feared that Moses would teach the people the true religion—Islam?

Pharaoh set his whole army against Moses only to be brought to aught.

"Pharaoh had deceived his slaves in the knowledge of Allah and the true religion (Islam), and indirectly had them worshipping him and his people as God.

Peace and Happiness

"The peace and happiness can't come to us under any other flag but our own.

"If God desires for us such joy, why shouldn't we give up begging and be real men, and sit with the rulers of the earth, ruling our own?

The Prodigal Son

"The other (Prodigal) son was so tempted by the loose life of strange women, drinking, gambling and adultery that it caused him to love the strangers' way of life, so much so that it cost him all that he originally possessed (self-independence and Divine guidance). His Father (God in Person) had to come and be his representative to again meet his brothers, family and friends.

The Holy Quran

"The Holy Quran was revealed to Muhammad in the seventh century A.D., over 1300 years ago, who spoke Arabic.

"The Holy Quran—it is holy because it is the Word of Allah (God), who speaks directly to His servant (Muhammad). 'Holy' means something that is PERFECTLY PURE, and this we just can't say of the poison Bible. Al-Quran means, according to the scholars of the language in which it is written, *that which should be read*. It was revealed (to Muhammad) in the month of Ramadan (2:185).

A Few Teachings of The Holy Quran

"Let us take a look at the opening of the second chapter of the Holy Ouran. Here Allah addresses Himself to us as being the Best Knower and that we must not entertain any doubts about the purity of His Book (the Holy Quran).

" 'I am Allah, the Best Knower. This book, there is no doubt in it, is a guide to those who guard (against) evil,' it says.

"Allah Himself speaks in the Holy Quran, not like the Bible which mentions 'Thus says the Lord'.

"In the Holy Quran, Allah challenges the disbelievers of our people and the devils combined to produce a chapter or even a verse like it. I quote another verse of the same chapter (2:285): 'The Apostle believes in what has been revealed to him from His Lord, and so do the believers; they all believe in Allah, His Angels, His Books, and His Apostles; We made no difference between any of the Apostles; and they (the believers) say, we hear and obey, our Lord; Thy forgiveness do we crave, and to Thee is the eventual recourse.'

"Can the proud Christians say with truth the same? No, they don't believe in Allah, not to mention His Prophets and the Scriptures of the Prophets, and they like to make a difference in the prophets. All the old prophets are condemned as being other than good, but Jesus they go to the extreme in making him a Son of God and (even) finally God. Yet they (also) say that they killed Jesus 'the Son of God' because he made himself the 'Son of God.'

Slave-Names

"He told us that we must give up our slavenames (of our slavemasters) and accept only the name of Allah (Himself) or one of the Divine attributes. We (the so-called Negroes) must also give up all evil doings and practices and do (only) righteousness or we shall be destroyed from the face of the earth."

I Do Not Make Mistakes

I do not make mistakes in what I write pertaining to these two races—black and white—and I do not need to study the theory of evolution to learn about them.

Theories do not always prove to be the truth. I have the truth from the All-wise One (Allah), to Whom praise is due. He has raised the curtain of falsehood which kept the true knowledge of the black and white races (especially the white race) from the peoples of the earth for 6,000 years.

They say that I am a preacher of racial hatred, but the fact is that the white people don't like the truth, especially if it speaks *against* them. This we have known all our lives.

Warning to My People

I warn you, my people, not to side with those who are against me and my followers, lest you find yourselves in the chastisement of Allah, the Almighty God. Allah and I are your friends; our enemies *cannot* be your friends. I am offering you LIFE eternally and our enemies are offering you slavery and death. Their own presidents, Congress and armies will not force their brothers to give you and I FREEDOM, JUSTICE and EQUALITY with them.

In many of their places they won't allow you to eat or drink, not even allow you into their public toilet facilities. They will also shoot you in some places if you dare ask for JUSTICE, and teach you to shoot the ones among you who seek JUSTICE for you.

It s a terrible thing for such people (Yakub's grafted race) to charge me with teaching race hatred when their feet are on my people's neck and they tell us to our face that they hate the black people —the so-called Negroes. Remember now, they even teach you that you must not hate them for hating you.

You Need Not Fear!

The so-called Negroes do not need to fear any more if they will believe in Allah (God) and follow me.

The Hog is Not a Food

The hog (pig) was made for the white race and for medical purposes only; regardless of who eats it, I say that it was not made to be taken as a food. On this point Allah and His Prophets are my witness, and are with me.

The Hog is Poison!

Now, of course, I do not care if *all* the white people eat the hog; I am only concerned with my people—the so-called Negroes—who don't know, nor do they understand. I know that not one of my poor people will go to Heaven (see the Hereafter) who eats this POISON HOG after being given the knowledge.

The Hog and Its Eaters

The white race knows that people eating swine flesh, committing acts of adultery, robbing, murdering and lying shall not be recognized as Servants of God and they won't see the Hereafter, unless, of course, they repent today. We see the white race in the South fighting to keep the so-called Negroes from even voting for one of their own (white people)) to rule them.

They even fight their own laws to prevent the so-called Negroes from sitting in classrooms with their children, although it is better even for *us* to not allow ourselves to be destroyed by mixing with them. Get an equal education, but stay to yourselves today. It is too late in the evening to try mixing the races.

Medical Science on Hog

The hog is called *khanzier* in the Arabic language, which means: *I see*

(khan) and *foul and very foul* (zier). This animal is indeed so foul, ugly and filthy that it is known to the medical profession that eating it decreases the mental power. There is a small opening in the inside of its front legs out of which flows a mass of corruption. The Medical Science says of this: "The opening is an outlet of a sewer." (See *MONITOR OF HEALTH*, by Dr. J. H. Kellogg, M.D.; pages 117-124)

The hog is completely shameless. Most animals have a certain amount of shyness, but not the hog, or his eater; they are similar. The hog-eater, it is a fact, will go nude in the public if allowed; his temper is easily aroused and under such conditions he will speak the ugliest, vilest, and most filthy language one has ever heard spoken in public. His mouth is full of cursing and swearing.

The hog is not a peaceful animal and can't get along in peace with others of his kind. He is the greediest of all animals. He will not divide his food with his young, except the milk in their bellies.

The hog is the cause, the very root of most of our sickness. STOP EATING IT and see for yourself.

Bible Forbids Eating of Hog

The Bible forbids you to eat the hog, Mr. Christian. It is forbidden by God through the mouth of His Prophets. Do you think that you can clear yourself with God by eating the swine and claiming it is all right?

I will give here some of the places in

your Bible where you can read of this Divinely-forbidden flesh (the hog). "Of their flesh shall you not eat, nor touch their dead carcass." (*Deut.*, 14:8) "I have spread out my hands all the day unto a rebellious people who eat swine's flesh and broth of abominable things is in their vessels." (*Isa.* 66:2) "In the heathen sacrifices some offered swine blood and burned incense to an idol." (*Isa.* 66:3) "They that sanctify themselves (call themselves sanctified and holy) in the Garden behind one tree (in the church behind its pastor) eating swine flesh, the abomination and the mouse, shall be consumed together, saith the Lord". (*Isa.* 66:18, where it also says: "Stand by thyself, come not near to me, for I am holier than thou." Such, of course, is said by hog-eating Christians!) Again it says in the same chapter: (66:5) "These are a smoke in my nose, a fire (anger) that burneth all the day."

In Mark, 5:11-16 it says: "Of their flesh thou shall not eat." Go and ask my followers who were once possessed with the devil and the swine how they feel since their release from such by Allah, to Whom praises are due.

The POISON SWINE is a scavenger and lives and thrives on filth, and the tissues of the hog are swarmed with parasites and worms which are 99 per cent poison. Allah has said: "They shall not eat the Swine." Says He in the Holy Quran, Chapter 2:168, 169, and 173: "O men, eat the lawful and good things out of what is in the earth, and do not follow in the footsteps of the devils." (The devils referred to are not other than the white people who eat the hog and other things forbidden by Allah.)

The devils (referred to in the Holy Quran) only enjoin upon you evil and indecency, and that you may speak against Allah and that which you do not know. When it is said to the so-called Negroes, "Follow what Allah has revealed." they says, "Nay, we follow what we found our fathers upon" though their fathers had no sense at all, nor did they follow the right way. He (Allah) has only forbidden to you what dies of itself, and the blood and the flesh of the filthy swine, and that over which any other name besides Allah has been invoked.

Allah says that the Caucasian race, having once been a savage people living in the caves and hillsides of Europe, ate almost everything like meat and ate it *raw* for 2,000 years. That was, to be exact, in the years before 4000 B.C. Naturally, they know good but just haven't the nature to do good, and you can't make them good unless they are returned into that which they were taken from. *You,* my people, who have the Divine Nature of God, do the things that are right. So *Unite, live and die for each other in the name of Allah and His Religion of Peace, Islam.* Do not let the Caucasians attract you to do evil things that you see them doing.

The One Hundred and Forty-four Thousand

This number is mentioned in the Bible (Rev. 14:1) as being the number of the first believers in Allah (God) and His messenger.

In that Chapter (Rev. 14:1) the messenger of God is called a lamb, due to certain characteristics of his (the messenger) being similar to that of a sheep, and the tender love of Allah for him is described like that of a good shepherd towards his sheep.

Now let us understand what we are reading. The number 144,000 is a prophecy about the future in symbolic terms and refers to a vision by Yakub, the father of the white race, which he had seen on the Isle of Patmos or Pelah 6,000 years ago. He was warning his people of that which would come to them at the end of their time.

The number 144,000 in mathematics means a SQUARE which is a perfect answer for the spiritual work of Allah with that number of people.

They are the first (Negro) converts from among the wicked to Allah (God) and His messenger, referred to as the first ripe fruit (the first of the righteous) unto God and the Lamb in verse 4 of the same chapter. They are righteous enough (ripe) to be picked out of the wicked race to be used for the purpose of squaring the nations of the earth into righteousness.

After the righteous black nation has labored under the wicked rule of the devils for 6,000 years, the return to a righteous ruler, under the God of Righteousness, the people must be re-organized to live under such government.

The All-Wise God, Allah, to Whom praise is due, Who came in the person of Master W. F. Muhammad, seeking us, the lost and last members of a chosen nation, is building a new world of Islam out of the old. Therefore, He lays the base of His Kingdom with a square number of mathematics which represents TRUTH.

His New World of Islam (Kingdom of Peace) can be proven mathematically step by step, and we all know that mathematics *is* Truth.

He (Allah) uses the square made of them (the so-called Negroes) whom He redeemed from among men (the Caucasian race); they were not defiled with women (the women other than their own kind).

This number will be made up of all the so-called American Negroes who have been the merchandise of the American whites for 400 years.

They now must be redeemed by Allah (God) for them to be free according to the Law of Justice, and become the servants of ther own God (Allah) again. The so-called Negroes should shout to learn of this Divine Truth.

The Revelator didn't see a single one of the Caucasian race in the number 144,000. He (Allah) gave the number of the beasts in the previous chapter (Rev. 13:18) as SIX, which is the true number of the Caucasion race or the Man of Sin.

The Bible says: "Let him that hath understanding count the number of beasts." After the coming of Allah (God), the symbolic beast and his number have been revealed, it is now understood.

The number 144: its root is 12 and

there are twelve tribes: the 12 Imams is the real answer.

Allah said that we once had 13 Tribes, but one got lost. The number 144 will be the Stars of the Nation, and this number (144) multiplied by 12 equals a cube.

This number (144,000) so-called Negroes, under the guidance of Allah (God), will cube the whole nation of black mankind into a nation of righteousness.

The Hereafter

What is meant by the Hereafter? It means, "After the destruction of the present world, its power and authority to rule." More specifically, it means, "After the present rule of the Man of Sin."

Some say that the Hereafter means "after the Judgement," that is, after the Man of Sin and his people have been judged and sentenced to death. I say that this present world was sentenced to death when the Man of Sin was made and all who follow him. It says in the Holy Quran (7:18), "Whoever of them will follow you, I will certainly fill hell with you all." The Bible says, "These both were cast alive into a lake of fire." (Rev. 19:20)

We all look forward to a Hereafter, to seeing and living under a ruler and a government of righteousness, after the destruction of the unrighteous.

The people of the Man of Sin (the devils) even are worried, disgusted and dissatisfied with their own world and wish to see a change to a better world;

but they desire to be the ruler in that Better World too, which they wouldn't be permitted by Allah.

Armageddon

Some believe the Hereafter means "after the Great War of Armageddon," which is a religious war between the two great religions of the earth—Islam and Christianity and their believers. Buddhism will also be involved in this (Great War of Armageddon).

What the Hereafter Will Be Like

The Righteous will make an unlimited progress in the Hereafter; peace, joy and happiness will have no end. Wars will be forgotten; there will be no place for disagreement.

The present Brotherhood of Islam is typical of the life in the Hereafter. The only difference is that the Brotherhood in the Hereafter will enjoy the spirit of gladness and happiness forever in the Presence of Allah.

There will be such a change in the general atmosphere of the earth (in the Hereafter) that the people will think it is a new earth. It will be the heaven of the righteous forever; no sickness, no hospitals, no insane asylums, no gambling, and no cursing or swearing will be seen or heard in that life. All fear, grief and sorrow will stop on this side as a proof.

The life in the Hereafter is an image

of the spiritual state in this life. Just think how good you feel when in the Divine Spirit for awhile—you are so happy that you don't feel even the pain of sickness, no trouble or sorrow, and that is the way you will feel always in the next life.

For My Followers, Hereafter is NOW!

Everyone of us—the so-called Negroes —who accepts the religion of Islam and follows what Allah has revealed to me will begin enjoying the above (Hereafter) life *here*, now!

Yes, the glorious joy and happiness is yours for the asking, my people. Accept Islam and see your God in truth, and the righteous will meet and embrace you with peace (As-Salaam-Alaikum).

You will be clothed in silk, interwoven with gold, and eat the best food that you desire. This is the time when you enter such life, for your God is here in Person, and you will never be that which you cannot be any more, after believing in Him.

Hereafter Not a Life of Spirits

My people have been deceived by the arch deceiver in regards to the Hereafter. They think the Hereafter is a life of spirits (spooks) up somewhere in the sky, while it is only on the earth, and you won't change to any spirit beings. The life in the hereafter is only a con-

tinuation of the present life. You will be flesh and blood. You won't see spooks coming up out of graves to meet God.

Read the Scriptures carefully on the life in the Hereafter, and try to understand their true meaning, and you will find that the Hereafter isn't what you have been believing. My people, no one is going to leave this planet to live on another; you can't even if you try! You can't reach the moon and live on it. So BE SATISFIED and BELIEVE IN ALLAH, live where you are on this good earth, but BE RIGHTEOUS.

Holy Quran on the Hereafter

The Holy Quran Sharrieff and the Bible are filled with readings on the Hereafter. Here I shall quote only these beautiful verses from the Holy Quran (89:27-30):

"O soul that is at rest, return to your Lord, well-pleased with Him, well-pleasing; So enter among My servants, and enter into My Paradise."

The Caucasian Race

I would like the Christians among my people, who say they are believers in the Bible and Jesus, to read and study the Chapter of John 8:42-44. It says in there, "If God was your Father, you would love me." If you understand it right, you will agree with me that the whole Caucasian race is a race of devils. They proved to be devils in the Garden of

Paradise and 4,000 years later they were condemned by Jesus. Likewise, they are condemned today by the Great Mahdi Muhammad as being nothing but devils in the plainest language.

Surely, if the Father of the two people (black and white) was the same, the two would love each other. In a family where the children are of one father, they love each other because they are of the same flesh and blood.

It is natural then for them to love each other. Again, it is not unnatural then for a member or members of a different race or nation not to love the non-member of their race or nation as their own.

The argument here (between Jesus and the Jews) is that the Jews claimed they all were the same people, children of one God (or Father), but this Jesus disagreed with and proved they were not from the same Father (God). He (Jesus), having a knowledge of both Fathers, knew their Father (Devil) before his fall and before he had produced his children (the white race) of whom the Jews are members. Here, in this Chapter (John 8), it shows there was no love in the Jews for Jesus.

Allah, Not Sword

The old Christian missionaries who wrote on the life and teachings of Muhammad, the Prophet, were his enemies. They were so grieved over the great success of Muhammad and Islam that they have written falsely against the man of God by attributing his success to the use of the sword instead of to Allah (God), from Whom it (Islam) actually came.

Muhammad and his followers were successful in their wars with their enemies because Allah, Whom they obeyed, was on their side. And Allah helped Muhammad and his followers because they fought for Truth and they were not the aggressors.

Here I might ask, is it the sword that is spreading Islam all over the world *today*, even here in America?

Self-Defense in Islam

The Holy Quran forbids "compulsory conversion" and teaches that a Muslim should never be the aggressor "but fight in the way of Allah with those who fight against you" (Chapter 2:190).

It is a Divine Law for us to defend ourselves if attacked. (May be if Jesus had let Peter and the other Desciples use the sword on the Jews he would have been more successful, for it was the sword that put him to death and the Jews remained disbelievers.)

Sword and Christianity

According to the Bible (Matthew 10: 34), Jesus didn't come for peace but to bring the sword. Neither did he come to unite. (Matthew 10:35) It stands true today that Christianity, as we see it in practice in America, certainly does not unite but rather divides the people against each other. According to the history of it, Christianity has caused more bloodshed than any other combination · of religions: its sword is never sheathed.

If Jesus was a peacemaker, then the Christians are not his followers.

"What have I done?"

This is a question often asked of me or of my followers by those who are not the Believers.

I am doing that for thousands (of my people) which Christianity failed to do —that is, uniting the so-called Negroes and making them to leave off evil habits that the preachers of Christianity haven't been able to do for a hundred years. We are that in Islam what Christianity offers beyond the grave.

Corruption in the World Today

"Corruption has appeared in the land and the sea, on account of what the hands of men have wrought," it says in the Holy Quran (Chapter 30:41).

How True! Corruption prevails everywhere on account of men's evil doings. Their hands, in fact, have built their own doom, and never before has such prophecy been fulfilled any clearer than today.

The world today is so evil and corrupted that people do not pay any attention to the preaching of good. Their hearts, minds, and souls are all going after evil and bloodshed of each other.

There is no peace among men; hatred and disagreement are universal. A change of religion must take place in order to save the nations from self-destruction. They (men) have corrupted the land and sea with all kinds of deadly arms— weapons of destruction which their hands have built.

They delight greatly in war but not in peace. Who then can enjoy peace in the midst of such a mad world? Who can be trusted? The alarm of war is heard and possibly designed to wipe mankind from the face of the earth. The land is charged with every type of man-made weapon of destruction of each other's lives. The sea is filled with deadly surface ships and undersea crafts (submarines). The sky has been filled with planes loaded with death to drop on our fellow-men. Yet they (men) say PEACE! Where is any peace with such evil forces free to spread death and destruction on the poor innocent human beings of the earth? They glory in killing and are not satisfied with the prosperity they have enjoyed. Their thanks to God is to destroy His people. This evil people have worked all of their lives making trouble, causing bloodshed among the peaceful people of the earth and themselves.

Their (this evil people's) greed in ruling the black people of the earth is unequaled. They send all their armed forces against you to make you bow to their rule. Even in your own home they want to rule according to their desire and not to yours, although it is your HOME.

Once they have access to enter your

28

house, they will go to war with you before they will leave in peace. They will take over your property and call it theirs. "Allah will scatter them who delight in war." (Psalm 69:30)

Let the world ponder — what does history show that the white man can call his own outside of Europe? However, they spread out and into the homes of black mankind of the earth, taking by armed force the black people's home and making slaves of them for many centuries.

The day has arrived for all coruption to end. It is the Day of Allah and the people of peace (believers in Allah) must have peace. The troublemakers must be punished and brought to an end so they will never be able to give trouble anymore.

Islam is Ageless and Will Last Forever

No one knows the age of Islam; it has no birth record. It will dominate mankind after the destruction of the devil, who is the sole troublemaker and disturber of black man's peace.

Islam first temporarily ceased to dominate mankind after the making of devil —6,000 years ago—who was then allowed to rule mankind. People began to divide themselves into families and tribes and set up their religions and objects of worship all over the earth. Allah (God) and His religion would not interfere with the rule of the devils and their false religion. If He *had* interfered,

there wouldn't have been any devils or a false religion today.

When Muhammad started teaching Islam in Arabia over 1300 years ago, just 600 years after the death of Jesus, he and his followers and successors almost converted the whole world back into Islam in a few hundred years. However, the re-conversion had to be slowed down to allow the devils to rule their time out. This has now taken place— the devils' time IS UP, and once again Islam is on the march, this time to never relax until all is under it or off the planet earth.

Not to mention the people of Gold Coast of West Africa only, but all black Africans are now turning to Islam. Go make an inspection for yourself, if you do not believe. Islam is now in America for the first time since the Red Indians came here 16,000 years ago, and it is here for the acceptance of the so-called Negroes whose fathers were once Muslims in their original home and who now are the last members of that chosen people to hear Islam, the Religion of Allah.

Slavery Among the Arabs

The Arabs are alleged to have slaves. The Arabs will answer for themselves, but I do know that no Muslim will enslave a Muslim. All Muslims are the brothers of another Muslim.

Any so-called Negro who turns Muslim can go and live among the Muslims of Arabia or anywhere on the planet earth and will be accepted as a brother and citizen of that government. Try it for yourself, brother. ALL ARE EQUAL IN ISLAM, not like your proud white Christians.

Why Not Islam for All Mankind?

The answer to this question ("Why not Islam for all Mankind?") is simple: All mankind can't believe and obey the teachings of Islam. All mankind are not members of the Righteous. Islam is righteousness and he who would believe in it and do the Will of Allah (God) must be by nature one born of Allah. The only people born of Allah is the Black Nation of which the so-called Negroes are descendants. That is why Islam is offered to them.

White Race Will Never Accept Islam

The white race, by nature, can't be righteous. Islam was taught to them from Moses to Muhammad, but they were never able to live the life of a Muslim believer and can't do it today. This fact the so-called Negroes must learn about the white race. They must learn that the white race cannot be righteous unless they could be born again (grafted back into the black man).

The poor, blind, deaf and dumb so-called Negroes work hard and live in hope that some day the white race will treat them right but this will never come to pass. And if they ever do treat them right, it will be against the will of that people. Certainly they can do it against their will but how long can such insincere love and justice last?

Words of Advice to My People

I advise you, my people, that, first of all, you will never be able to live as you desire — in freedom, justice and equality — until you are in your own (Islam).

Whatever profession or trade you may have, do something for yourself and your kind and choose for yourself the one religion (Islam). Islam alone will secure for you favor and protection of Allah, also universal Brotherhood.

Stop looking for anything after death —Heaven or Hell. These are in *this* life. Death settles it all.

Stop eating yourself to death by eating three meals a day. Eat once a day and eat the best food, which when eaten correctly, keeps you in the best of health. Stay away from the HOG meat. Don't eat stale beef, chicken or fish. Eat fresh products.

Don't eat field peas such as brown or black-eyed peas and lima beans. Don't eat collard greens, cabbage sprouts, cornbread. Eat brown bread (whole wheat) and butter, if not over-weight, and a little cheese. Drink milk. Cook your food well done.

Pray five times a day with your face toward the east.

Love your black brother as thyself. Do good to all.

Muslim Names are Beautiful

All Muslim names are beautiful and have a beautiful meaning. Ninety-nine per cent of them are divine attributes (of Allah). Remember, my people, Jones, Johnson, Smith, Hog, Bird, Fish, Bear, Woods, and such names as Roundtree will not be accepted by Allah, your God and mine.

ISLAM – The Original Religion

Islam is the original religion of *all* black mankind. There is no doubt about it, according to the meaning of Islam and what the Holy Quran Sharrieff teaches us of it. Islam means peace and submission to the will of Allah (God), who is the Author of Islam.

ISLAM – The Religion of All the Prophets

The name "Islam" is not an invented one, as is the case with other religions. The name of our religion comes from Allah Himself, and is the religion of all the Prophets of Allah, including Abraham, Moses, Jesus and Muhammad, the Last of His Prophets. Says the Holy Quran, "Surely the True Religion with Allah is Islam."

ISLAM – The Religion of Peace

Islam means peace, therefore it is the Religion of Peace. Could we imagine Allah giving mankind any other religion but one of peace? Or could we imagine a prophet of Allah bringing us a religion other than of peace? Certainly not.

ISLAM in the Bible

It is Islam, the Religion of Peace, and none other, that God offers us in the Bible (Num. 6:26; Ps. 29:11-85:8: and Is. 26:3-32:17). There are many other places in the Bible that prove that Islam, the Religion of Peace, is mentioned as being the religion of Allah (God).

ISLAM – The Religion of the Tribe of Shabazz

The religion of the whole tribe of Shabazz was none other than Islam. It was also the religion of Yakub, the father of the white race, before his fall.

ISLAM – The Perfect Religion

Allah says of Islam in the Holy Quran "This day I have perfected for you a religion; completed my favor on you and chose for you Islam as a religion." (Chapter 5:3)

Slavemasters' Educational System Won't Help Us

Recently one of my people who is other than a Believer wrote to me and boasted about our "having some of the finest schools" and mentioned a few well-known names as "proof" of the "great progress" my people have made in America in recent years.

But is it not true, my people, that your schools, colleges and universities are from the slavemasters? And who is benefitted by the graduates of these schools — the white man or the so-called Negroes?

I say that regardless of how much education your slavemasters give you, if they never teach you a true knowledge of self, you are only a free slave to serve them or others than your own.

Is your present educational system getting you independence from the slavemasters' children? Is it or has it put the idea in your head to seek some of this good earth for you and your people, who number over 17 million in America, and a place to call your own? NO!

Who appoints your men to degrees and scientists to high government posts? Is it not their white masters whom they are going to serve? You will seek white men's jobs, but not a country for your people.

Home of Your Own

I want to see you, my people, in a country that you can call your own and where your highly trained and educated men and women can be benefitted. May Allah and Islam give it to you. There is no hope for such under the slavemaster's children and their flag.

Too Many Gods?

Some of my people say that "the trouble with us is that we have too many Gods." Then why not believe in One God (Allah) and we all will be trouble-free?

Know the Truth, My People!

Because my people, the so-called Negroes, know so little about themselves and know so little of the treachery of the many other racial groups, we suffer untold human indignities in order to obtain so-called "eqaulity" of opportunity in public accomodations, schools, churches, sports, etc. We seek to be accepted as members of the white slavemaster's family. And regardless of the savage treatment we receive, we pour out our life-blood like water to be near our enemies. May Allah open my people's eyes that they may see and know the Truth!

If they only knew the Truth, they would prefer sitting as far removed from their enemies as the East is from the West.

Know the Truth, my people, and return to your God, Allah, and His Religion, Islam, that I may protect you and save you.

32

How Islam Benefits Us

The religion of Islam makes one think in terms of self and one's own kind. Thus, this kind of thinking produces an industrious people who are self-independent. Christianity does just the opposite: makes the so-called Negroes lazy, careless and dependent people.

Think over such slavery teachings as this: "That a rich man can't see the hereafter," and compare it with the promise of Allah who offers the righteous Heaven (riches) while they are alive.

I must continue to warn you that you can't depend on the white race to care for you forever. There has got to be an end to your dependence on them. So, why not start in time seeking something for self?

Know this, my people, that this is the fall and end of the white race as a dominant power on the earth, and that the loss of Asia (alone) to the white race means the end of their luxury.

It must come to pass, believe it or not! So get on to your kind and be benefitted by Islam.

In Heaven Overnight!

If the so-called American Negroes would try living in unity, have love for self and their kind (the Black Man) they would be in Heaven overnight!

Islam Alone Can Unite the So-Called Negroes

It is a great job trying to change the so-called Negroes from the ways of their slavemasters and to unite them. It may take much suffering but I say that it CAN be done. Islam will unite us all. I know Christianity can't unite us; instead, it divides us. That is what it was intended to do, to divide people.

History of the Tribe of Shabazz

It is Allah's will and purpose that we shall know ourselves; therefore, He came Himself to teach us the knowledge of self. Who is better knowing of whom we are than God Himself? He has declared that we are descendants of the Asian black nation and of the tribe of Shabazz.

You might ask, who is this tribe of Shabazz? Originally, they were the tribe that came with the earth (or this part of it) sixty trillion years ago when a great explosion on our planet divided it into two parts. One we call earth, the other moon.

We, the tribe of Shabazz, says Allah (God), were the first to discover the best part of our planet (earth) to live on, which is the rich Nile Valley of Egypt and the present seat of the Holy City, Mecca, Arabia.

Kinky Hair

The origin of our kinky hair came from one of our dissatisfied scientists, fifty thousand years ago, who wanted to make all of us tough and hard in order to endure the life of the jungles of East

Asia (Africa) and to overcome the beasts there. But he failed to get the others to agree with him. He took his family and moved into the jungle to prove to us that we could live there and conquer the wild beasts and we have.

White Race's Day is Over

I must keep warning you that you should give up the white race's names and religion in order to gain success. Their days of success are over; their rule will last only as long as you remain asleep to the knowledge of self.

Awake and know that Allah has RE-VEALED the Truth. Stop believing in something coming to you after you are physically dead. That is untrue and no one can show you any proof of such belief.

Jesus Cannot Hear You Pray

Know that Jesus was only a prophet and cannot hear you pray any more than Moses or any other dead prophet. Allah alone can hear your prayers and answer them.

Islam, and Nothing Else but Islam

Why do I stress the religion of Islam for my people, the so-called Negroes?

First, and most important of all: Islam *is* actually *our* religion by nature.

It is the religion of Allah (God) and not an European-organized white man's religion.

Second: It is the original, *the only* religion of Allah (God) and His prophets. It is also the only religion that will save the lives of my people and will give them divine protection against our enemies.

Third: Islam dignifies the black man. It gives him the desire to be clean, internally and externally, and to have, for the first time, a sense of dignity.

Fourth: Islam removes fear and makes one FEARLESS; it educates us into the knowledge of God and the devil, which is so necessary for my people.

Fifth: It makes us to know and love one another as never before.

Sixth: Islam destroys superstition and removes the veil of falsehood. It heals both the physical and spiritual by teaching what to eat, when to eat, and what to think, and how to act.

Seventh: It is the only religion that has the Divine power to unite us and save us from the destruction of the War of Armageddon, which is now. It is also the only religion in which the Believer is really divinely protected, and the only religion that will survive the Great Holy War, or the final war between Allah (God) and the devil.

I say, therefore, Islam and nothing else but Islam is meant to solve the so-called Negroes' problems and raise them from their mentally-dead condition. Islam in fact, will put the black man of America on top of the civilization.

Other Notable Aspects of Islam

There are, of course, many other notable and worthy aspects of Islam my people should know about.

Islam, for instance, makes hell and heaven not two places but two *conditions of life*, which is very easy to understand. For there could never be either unless it was brought about by our own efforts or making. The earth is our home and we can make it a hell or heaven for us. If we follow and obey Allah and His prophets, we make it a heaven. If we follow and obey the devil and his prophets, we make it a hell.

Islam brings about a peace of mind and contentment to the believer, and for the first time, love for our own black brothers and sisters. What one loves for himself, he must love for his brother. I will say here that this alone is salvation to you and me, just learning to love each other as brothers. Islam, unlike Christianity, is doing this right *in your midst*.

Regardless to how long and how hard you try to be a good Christian, you never have a sincere, true love for your own black brother and sister as you should. Islam will give you true brothers and sisters the world over, and this is what you need.

A people subjected to all kinds of injustices need to join Islam, as you are sure of Allah's help in Islam. Why don't the preachers of my people preach Islam? If they would, overnight they could be on top.

Leave Your False Pride Now and Accept Allah

Are you proud to submit to Allah (God) and sit in Heaven while you live, and have His protection against your open enemy? Then that is false pride and you should lose no time in shedding it. Take it or leave it, but you will soon wish that you had submitted to Allah. God is drying America up by degrees, little by little, and hell is kindling up. Islam *is* the right way for you, so join up the Brotherhood now.

The Faithful's Mark

To be truthful with you, God has said to me, He will not accept any white people in His Kingdom. A special mark will distinguish the righteous from the devils, and it will be in their foreheads caused by prostrating. The Muslims prostrate in their prayers on rough floors or rugs, which produces a mark on their forehead. (Some of my followers have such a sign now, produced by the five-prayers-a-day obligation.) The righteous is always marked by his righteousness, as the wicked is marked by his or her wicked acts. They are actually marked by nature and are recognized by both parties.

Resurrection of the Dead

You, who believe literally in the physical resurrection of the dead, must remember the Bible (Rev. 14:4) teaches that the first reighteous to be

35

saved (the 144,000) are redeemable from among men, not out of the grave. It is a sin that you are so blinded that you cannot see, nor will you accept plain TRUTH. Surely, there is a resurrection of the dead. It is one of the principles of Islam, but not the physically dead in the graveyards. It is the mentally dead, th ignorant, whom the devil's falsehood has killed, to the knowledge of truth, the DIVINE TRUTH. This TRUTH must now be preached to them to awaken them into the knowledge of Him again. You and I know that it can't refer to a physically dead person, because that one won't and can't rise again. What is left to rise from a body that has gone back to the earth, or up in moke, or eaten by some wild beast or fish of the sea? What about the people who died before the flood and after? Even Adam? They have nothing to rise from. Remember, the old Testament (the Torah) doesn't teach of a resurrection of the dead, according to Job (chapter 7:9), wherein it says "He that goeth down to the grave shall come up no more." He must be right as we haven't seen one come up yet from the grave that was really dead. Surely, if it had meant a physical death God would have taught it to Adam, Noah, Abraham, Moses and all of the ancient phophets would have had a knowledge of it, even Job, but not so is the case.

The So-Called Negroes are Good by Nature

The so-called Negroes (descendants of the Tribe of Shabazz) are good people and very religiously inclined *by nature*. However, it is for the FIRST TIME that they are hearing of and accepting "the right religion in the right state," as it is stated in the Holy Quran. Islam, the religion of Allah, IS the religion of the so-called Negroes, though their enemies may be adverse.

My people, in fact, are inclined to righteous worship so much so that they are constantly seen disgracing themselves in their ignorant way, due to the lack of knowledge of their God and His True Religion, Islam.

For the past 100 years since the slavemasters have opened the doors of their (Christian) church to them, they have gone insane over it. They have not taken a sane thought that if there were any saving power in the white race's churches of Christianity for them, why hasn't the POWER freed them from the slavemasters' children? Why are they begging them now for civil rights, which are supposedly given to any citizen by the Constitution? A slave or a free slave is not his master's equal. It is, therefore, silly for the so-called Negroes to think of being granted equal rights with their slavemasters' children.

Think of it!—They are a people who beg you to become a member of their Christian church and after accepting it with your whole heart, then you must pray to them for recognition! They are ashamed to even call you a brother or sister in their religion and their very nature rebels against recognizing you!

36

Islam Recognizes Equality of Brotherhood; Christianity Does Not

Islam recognizes complete equality of Brotherhood; a Muslim is truly the brother of another Believer, regardless of how black the skin or how kinked the hair. He is welcomed with sincere and open arms and recognized by his light-skinned or copper-colored Arab brother. He is also recognized in the same way by his brown or yellow-skinned Japanese, Chinese and Indian brothers. Can you say this for your Christianity, my people? No, your slavemasters' religion does not recognize equality of brotherhood.

In Islam, in fact, you are not a believer until you first love for your brother that which you love for yourself.

If the white Christians had meant good for you and me, why did they make slaves of us, and why are they still subjecting us to the most severe and ugliest injustices?

"Right Religion in the Right State"

I' have used this expression before, which is a quotation from the Holy Quran. I shall now explain what this expression exactly means:

A religion is in the "right state" when its author is the All Righteous Being (Allah) and it is believed and practiced according to His will. It must also apply to our nature in which we were born. That, then, is the "right religion in the right state."

It is Natural to Love Freedom and Justice

It is entirely natural for man to want to be equal of man. It is natural, again, for man to love the Brotherhood of Man (except the man devil).

Further, it is natural for man to love FREEDOM for himself, for Freedom is essential to life, and to love JUSTICE for himself, for without Justice there is no joy in freedom and equality.

Can you say, my people, that you are enjoying freedom, justice and equality in Christianity?

The Signs of Islam

Islam is most surely the "right religion in the right state." Here is another proof:

Islam uses for its Signs the Sun, Moon and the Star. These three elements (of Nature) are most essential for our well-being, and they represent a physical work of Freedom, Justice and Equality.

The Sign of Christianity

The Cross (the sign or emblem) of Christianity represents the physical workings of that religion. The Cross is far from being a sign of a true religion. If a religion's base (foundation) or sign is not found in the universal order of things, it cannot be called the religion of Allah (God), nor can it be called a "religion in the right state."

My people, the so-called Negroes, should never wear a cross as a sign for his or her salvation, for it is just the opposite.

Who is the Original Man?

This question (Who is the Original Man?) is being answered from the mouth of Allah (God) to us (the so-called Negroes) for the first time since our straying away from our own nation.

This secret of God and the devil has been a mystery to the average one of mankind, and it has now been revealed in all its clearness to one who was so ignorant that he knew not even himself, born blind, deaf, and dumb in the wildernes of North America.

The truth about the devil is now being told and taught throughout the world, to his anger and deep sorrow. He is losing no time trying to hinder this truth of the above question, "Who is the Original Man?

The devil, in fact, is setting watchers and listeners around me and my followers to see if he can find some other charge to put against us to satisfy his anger at the truth that we preach which is from the mouth of Allah, who is with us in Person.

The Original Man, Allah has declared, is none other than the black man. He is the first and the last, and maker and owner of the universe; from him come all — brown, yellow, red and white. By using a special method of birth control law, the black man was able to produce the white race.

The true knowledge of the black and white mankind should be enough to awaken the so-called Negroes, put them on their feet and on the road to self-independece. Yet, they are so afraid of the slavemasters that they even love them to their destruction and wish that the bearer of Truth would not tell it (the Truth) even if he knows it.

The time has arrived when it must be told the world over who the Original Man is, for there are millions who do not know it. Why should this question be put before the world today? Because it is the TIME OF JUDGEMENT between the two (black and white) people, and to be without the knowledge of the Original Man means to be without the knowledge of the rightful owner of the earth.

History of the Original Man

Allah (to Whom praise is due) is now pointing out to the nations of the earth their rightful places and this judgement will bring an end to *wars* over it.

Now it is so easy to recognize the Original Man, the real owner of the earth, by the history of the two (black and white) people. We have an unending past history of the black nation and a limited one of the white race.

We find that history teaches that the earth was populated by the black nation ever since it was created, but the history of the white race doesn't take us beyond 6,000 years.

Everywhere the white race has gone on our planet, he either found the Original Man or a sign that he had been there previously. Allah is proving to the world of black man that the white race actually doesn't own any part of our planet.

The Bible as well as the Holy Quran bear witness to the above fact, if you are able to understand it.

The Knowledge of White Race Removes All Misunderstanding

A true knowledge of the white race removes once and for all times the mistakes that would be made in dealing with them. My followers and I can and are getting along with them in a more understandable way than ever, because we know them.

You can't blame one for the way he or she was born, for they had nothing to do with that. Can we say to them why don't you do righteousness when Nature did not give righteouness to them? Or can we say to them why are you such a wicked devil? Who is responsible—the made or the maker?

(The white man did not make himself.)

Yet this does not excuse us for following and practicing his evil habits or accepting him for a righteous guide just because he is not his maker.

Spiritual Civilization

The duty of a civilized man is to teach civilization and the arts and sciences of civilized people to the uncivilized.

The duty of a Divine Messenger, raised by Allah Himself, is to teach his people spiritual civilization, which is important and necessary for the success of a society. According to history, the people who refuse to accept Divine Guidance or Allah's Message brought by His Messengers are classified as uncivilized or savages.

A well-educated, cultured and courteous people make a beautiful society when it is spiritual. Good manners come from the civilized man who doesn't fail to perform his duty.

Types of Civilization

There are several civilizations; we have a wicked one and a righteous one. It is a righteous civilization that is in the workings now. We all have been well-trained into the wicked civilization; now we must be trained into the knowledge of the righteous one. We MUST have a righteous-trained, civilized man, who will not fail to perform

39

his duty to us in guiding and teaching us.

The Righteous Civilization

My people in America, the so-called Negroes, are under the searchlight of the righteous, who are offering to them the right guidance to supreme civilization of righteousness, never witnessed before on earth. The white race has failed to perform its duty of civilizing the American so-called Negroes. Of course, they have been their slaves for many centuries, and the slavemasters have rights over them, as long as they are (the slavemasters') slaves. However, if the slavemasters free their slaves—not in words but in deeds—the slavemasters should provide the once-slaves with the right civilization and with everything necessary for them to start an INDE-PENDENT life as their slavemasters have.

Certainly, the so-called Negroes are being schooled, but is it the equal of their slavemasters? No, the so-called Negroes are still begging for equal education. After being blinded to the knowledge of self and their own kind for 400 years, the slavemasters refuse to civilize the so-called Negroes into the knowledge of themselves of which they were robbed. The slavemasters also persecute and hinder anyone who tries to perform this most rightful duty.

I will continue to say that as long as the so-called Negroes don't know who they really are and do not have the knowledge to free themselves from their slavemasters' names and religion, they can't be considered civilized.

Nothing in a Name?

Some of the so-called Negroes are ignorant to the important advantage of having their own nation's names. They think there is nothing to a name. I say they are right, but only in regard to the names they are NOW using, and not in regard to their own nation's names which they don't have. The Bible says, "A good name is better than gold." To continue to bear the slavemasters' names makes them the property of their slavemasters and they can never hope to receive equal recognition in the civilized world.

The Right Path for My People

It has been seen from the little chance my people have had to get a little education and they have shown and proven that they ARE the ORIGINAL PEOPLE, who are only asleep and in great need of the right civilized man who will perform his duty of awakening them. The so-called Negroes' fear of being deprived of food, clothing and shelter, also the usual smile of the white slavemasters' children prevents them from seeking the true knowledge of their own nation's civilization.

I say that they MUST drop the

slavemasters' names and religion, because both of these mean nothing but continued slavery. If they would understand, there is no other RIGHT PATH for my people.

Of course, some (not all) preachers and politicians, who live off the ignorance of their people, are opposed to the right civilization of our people (the so-called ' Negroes). These are the people who teach the so-called Negroes) to eat the wrong food and to drink, to indulge in games of chance (gambling), to go half-dressed, and to look for salvation *after death* (and not give a hoot for salvation in *this life*, as right civilization teaches us). Their teachings, my people, are not for your good.

Come and follow the Right Path and the RIGHT GUIDE, and be rightly civilized.

Separation from the Slavemasters is a Must

You, my people, must know that you have not been rightly civilized. No one can enslave another who has equal education(Knowledge). My people lack science (knowledge) of the right kind.

Allah (to Whom praise is due) is now here to give you and me a superior knowledge of things and a country to ourselves. Separation of the so-called Negroes from their slavemasters' children is a MUST. It is the only SOLUTION to our problem. It was the only solution, according to the Bible, for Israel and the

Egyptians, and it will prove to be the only solution for America and her slaves, whom she mockingly calls her citizens, without granting her citizenship. We must keep this in our minds at all times that we are actually being mocked.

I think it is a DISGRACE to us for ever bing .satisfied with only a servant's part. Should not we, as a people, want for ourselves what other civilized nations have?

The Prophecy about the 144.000

It is written (Rev. 14:1) that only 144,-000 of us will accept and return to our God (Allah) and the rest, 16,856,000, would go down with His enemies. For this sad prophecy of the loss of my people, I write what I am writing, hoping perhaps that you may be able to beat the old prophets' prediction by making the truth so simple that a fool can understan it.

You must be rightly civilized. You must go back to your OWN PEOPLE and COUNTRY, but not one of you can. return with what you have. You must know that this is the Time of Judgement of this World (of the Caucasian race) that you and I have known. Therefore, Allah has said to me that the Time of is ripe for you and me to accept our own (the whole Planet Earth).

What are YOU waiting for—the destruction ? Come, let us reason together. (But *you* cannot reason until you have a thorough knowledge oof self). Who are you waitng on to teach you to the knowledge? (The white man's civilization will never work for us.)

Poison Foods

Allah (God) has blessed America (not because she is good) with plenty of good eatables—millions of pounds of beef, lamb, chicken and fish of all kinds are available at all times. Yet she eats the dirty and filthy hog, to Allah's dislike, and almost forces the so-called Negroes to eat it, or I would say everyone. America drinks more alcohol—forbidden by Allah—than anyone else. She is blessed with so much wheat that she can hardly find room to store it, and will even burn it to raise the price, yet she teaches the so-called Negroes to eat CORNBREAD and the HOG, both of which are a slow death to my people in the soutern parts of this country.

My people have been reared on such POISON FOODS and now all the doctors in the world can't tell them that it is not good for them.

The hogs contain trichina (called pork worms) whose larvae infest the intestines and muscles of hog-eaters. This animal (hog) is one of Allah's most hated and it was never intended to be eaten.

Is There a Mystery God?

Who is the MYSTERY GOD? We should take time and study what has and is being taught to us. Study the words "Mystery God" and examine them, and if it be the Truth, lay hold to it.

To teach people that God is a "Mystery God" is to teach them that God is UNKNOWN. There is no truth in such a teaching. Can one teach which he himself does not know?

The word "Mystery," according to the Englis dictionaries, is: "something that has not been or cannot be," or "something beyond human comprehension." The unintelligent, or rather ones without divine knowledge, seem to delight themselves in representing that God is something mysterious (UNKNOWN). I say that such teaching makes the prophets' teaching of God all false.

According to Allah, the origin of such teaching as a mystery God is from the the devils; it was taught to them by their father, Yakub, 6,000 years ago. They know today that God is not a mystery, but will not teach the Truth about it. He (devil), the god of evil, was made to rule the nations of earth for 6,000 years and naturally he would not teach obedience to a God other than himself

So, a knowledge of the true God of Righteousness was not represented by the devils. The true God was not to be made manifest to the people until the God of evil (devil) had finished or lived out his time which was allowed him to deceive the nations. (Read Thessalonians 2:9-10 and Rev. 20:3-8-10).

The shutting up and loosening of the devil mentioned in Rev. 20:7, could refer to the time between the A.D. 570-1555 when John Hawkins (and others) deceived our foreparents in Africa and brought them into slavery in America. That's nearly 1,000 years that they and Christianity were bottled up in Europe by the spread of Islam by Muhammad (may the peace of Allah be upon him!) and his successors.

Their being loose to deceive the nations of the earth would refer to the time A.D. 1555 to 1955, during which they were loose (free) to travel over the earth and deceive the people.

Now their (the devils') freedom is being interfered with, by the Order and Power of the God of Righteous through the Nation of Righteous.

Allah is Here, in Person!

For the past 6,000 years, the prophets have been predicting the coming of God who would be Just and Righteous...This Righteous God would appear at the end of the world (of the white race).

Today, the God of Truth and Righteousness is making Himself manifest. He is not any more a mystery (unknown), but is KNOWN and can be SEEN and HEARD the earth over.

The teaching of God being a mystery has so enslaved the minds of my poor, ignorant people and they are so pitifully blind, deaf and dumb that it hurts; but I am going to prove to them that I am with Allah (God) and that He (Allah) is with me.

In spite of their (my people's) ignorance of Allah and myself whom He has sent—for I am not self-sent—they and the world shall soon know who it is that has sent me.

God is here in Person, so stop looking for a dead Jesus for help and pray to HIM whom Jesus prophesied that would come after him. My, people, pray to the One who is ALIVE and not a spook!

Islam Will Replace All Other Religions

"He it is who sent His Apostle with the guidance and the True religion that he make it overcome the religions, all of them, though the polytheists may be averse." (The Holy Quran, 61:9)

In the above verse Allah (God) in the last days of this present world (of wicked infidels) states that He must destroy false religions with the True Religion Islam. It (Islam) must overcome all other religions.

That also means, as is indicated by the true meaning of the above verse, that Allah in the judgement of the world will definitely NOT RECOGNIZE any religion other than Islam.

Take to task all the learned teachers of religions and they will admit that God IS One and that He will have only one religion in the Hearafter—Islam—which will replace all other religions.

All Opposition to Islam Will Vanish

Search the Scriptures of the Bible and Holy Quran, and these will tell you that ultimately all opposition to Islam will vanish.

There are today two other religions

which are opposed to the religion of peace, Islam. These are Buddhism and Christianity. With the help of Allah, these two opponents of Islam will be so completely eradicated from the planet earth that you won't even find a trace of them.

I say that Christianity is *already* dying a natural death.

The Light of Islam Will Shine Forever

"They desire to put out the light of Allah with their mouths, but Allah will perfect His light though the unbelievers may be averse," it says in the Holy Quran (61:8).

It means that regardless of the efforts (of the devil) to put out the light of Truth (Islam) today, it will continue to shine the world over, and forever!

Christianity, Budhism and Islam

What a difference there is between the three religions!

The first teaches that there are three Gods, not one. It also requires worship of Mary, mother of Jesus, and of the desciples of Jesus. The second, Buddhism, requires belief in "re-carnation," and contains many ignorant practices.

Islam, on the other hand, is entirely free of confusing doctrines and of ignorant practices.

It (Islam) teaches an eternal heaven for the righteous. (Hell, according to Islam, is not eternal.)

It (Islam) also teaches that if a brother kills a brother the murderer must be killed, on anyone that murders a Muslim (must be killed).

Why Islam' Must Overcome Other Religions?

The answer to this question is very simple: Because Islam is the only religion of Allah, and He (Allah) has declared (in the Holy Quran) that Islam MUST overcome all other religions which are not from Him.

This also proves the point that if the religions other than Islam were true (religions) surely Allah would not send an Apostle to overcome them with another religion (Islam).

It says in the Holy Quran, "Is it other than Allah's religion that they seek to follow, and to Him submits whoever is in the heavens and on earth, willingly or unwillingly." (3:82) We bear witness to the TRUTH that everything of Allah's creation obeys Him, regardless of size or numbers.

Muslim's Prayers

Muslims pray five times a day, not once a week or once a year.

They pray at sunrise, at noon, mid-aftrenoon, at sundown, and before retiring.

44

If awakened through the night, another prayer is made! In fact, two prayers should be said during the night, making a total of seven prayers a day.

There is no worship of a Sunday or Sabbath in Islam, all the days are worship days.

The Muslims wash and clean all exposed parts of their bodies before each prayer, which is made facing in the direction of the SUNRISE (East).

Muslim Prayer Service is Unequaled

Study the Muslim's way of worship and you will agree with me that there is no better way of divine worship. Why? For one thing, the Muslim always washes and cleans himself before communicating with Allah (God). In other words, he first cleans his own body and *then* invites the clean Holy Spirit to come (into his body). That is the best state (of body as well as of mind) in which to say one's prayers.

Ablution

The process of bodily cleanliness which precedes the Muslim's prayers is known as Ablution. Here is how it is performed:

The Muslim first washes his hands, then he rinses his mouth. Then he washes his arms, up to the elbows (if exposed). Ablution is completed by washing the feet.

The Significance of Ablution

Each part of the Ablution requirement has some significance. For instance, the Muslim washes his hands to "get rid of any evil" they might have committed. This also signifies that the Muslim thus asks Allah to wash his hands in the Spirit of Forgiveness.

Mecca, the Holy City

When the Muslim has performed his Ablution, (which means also that his hands are now spread forth, his ears cleaned from the hearing of evil, and eyes closed from seeing evil,) he then steps on his prayer rug or mat, and faces toward the ONLY HOLY SPOT on our planet— the Holy City of Mecca.

Abraham and Ishmael

Mecca is the Holy City wherein Abraham had made an attempt to sacrifice his son Ishmael, under a trial of Allah (God), which was also a sign of what would take place in the Last Days on finding and returning the lost-found people of Abraham an his son, Ishmael.

Description of Prayer

The Muslim begins his prayer by declaring that ALLAH IS THE GREATEST and that he bears witness that there is "No God but ALLAH," and that none deserves to be served (worshipped) but

(There is but one God ; Muhammad is His messenger)

Him. He further declares that Muhammad is His Last Apostle (an Apostle whom Allah would raise from the lost and found people of the seed of Abraham in the Days of Judgement).

After this the Muslim declares: "I have turned myself to Allah, being upright to Him who originated the Heavens and the Earth. I am indeed not one of the polytheists." (A polytheist is one who believes in more than one God.)

Muslim Prayer Service Best Suits the So-Called Negroes

I say that no religious worshipper could beat such a preparation for his prayer service or use more honor and submission to his Maker as I have described in preceding paragraphs.

The Muslim's Prayer Service, therefore, is the best to be used by the so-called Negroes in America, for its words fit *their* condition more than any other people on earth.

Until now, we have been turned from our God (Allah) towards the devil, believing in and worshipping a trinity of Gods, with our faces down or upward towards the sky, and our thoughts of God in the sky.

Meaning of the Various "Steps" of Muslim's Prayer

The various "steps" of the Muslim's prayer — turning, bowing, sitting, and prostrating — all have a beautiful meaning, which space won't allow me (to explain) here.

The Muslims are in accord with the whole Earth's turning; the Earth revolves on·its axis eastward toward the Sun, being attracted by it. Eastward is where we look to daylight, and it is in that direction wherefrom came the prophets and civilization of man.

Again, it is the East from which direction we were told to expect the coming of the Son of Man (God in Person) in the last days of the wicked.

The Significance of the Seven Prayers

The Muslim is required to pray five times a day, and twice at night if he awakens. This totals seven. What is the significance of this number seven?

Do we not have seven inhabited planets? And a Seven-thousandth year after the six thousand years of the devil's rule?

Are we not reminded of this in the six work days of the week (the six thousand years of the workings of the devils) and the seventh to rest which belongs to the Lord (the original owners, the Black Man)?

Muslim's Oft-Repeated Prayer

The Muslim's oft-repeated prayer is as follows:

"In the Name of Allah, the Beneficent, the Merciful. All Praise is due to Allah, the Lord of the Worlds; the Beneficent, the Merciful; Master of the Day of Requital. Thee do we serve, and Thee do we beseech for help. Guide us on the Right Path — the path of those upon whom Thou hast bestowed favors, not of those upon whom Thy wrath is brought down, nor of those who go astray."

Through this beautiful prayer the Muslim seeks the Path to trod that will bring him Divine help, and for the so-called Negroes ISLAM is that path which will get Divine help on their side.

My people, set you face upright for the religion in the right state — Islam!

"The Great is Falling"

"The Great is Falling. Come out of her, my people, that you be not partakers of her sins and receive not of her plagues," it says in the Bible (Rev. 18:2,4).

The so-called Negroes know not that the above warnings are directed to them, and they are living in the country where all the prophecies of this chapter have been and are being fulfilled.

Why should the Great Babylon fall? The second verse answers that: Because she has become the HABITATION OF DEVILS and the hold of every FOUL SPIRIT and a cage of every unclean and Hateful Bird (Rev. 18:2). Nothing could fit the description of North America better, and my poor spiritually-blinded people do not know it.

North America is the habitation of every type of human wickedness. Ancient Sodom, Gomarrah, Nineveh, Babylon and Roman sins were only children's acts compared with the modern sins of America. The wicked cry and rage for more freedom to commit more sins.

They practice the worst kind of filthy wickedness that takes scientists to think up and invent. This people have done and will do worse.

after being engulfed into the Divine chastisement.

America, the Modern Babylon

America is the Babylon of today.

Gambling is a common sin here, together with drunkenness, use of drugs, adultery, loving of self, sweethearting with one's own sex, and murder.

Sodom was rich and her people passed away their time in idleness, but it cannot be compared with the Modern Babylon. Her equal is not found in the past.

I say that America committed suicide when she brought the so-called Negroes from their native land and into slavery. This can't be forgiven her, though the so-called Negroes would gladly forgive for promise of social equality. But it is not left to the slave to forgive his master.

The Parables of Lazarus and the Rich Man

Remember the Bible's parables of Lazarus and the rich man, and Abraham acting as the spokesman for Lazarus? Abraham knew that Lazarus would have been foolish enough to try making an attempt to save his master who was in hell to his own destruction. Not one time did the rich man ask Abraham to bring him water, but he knew the weakness of his servant Lazarus, and was fully aware of the consequences of Lazarus' attempt to aid him

The Great Mahdi

In Rev. (18:1) it says that the Revelator saw an angel come from Heaven (from the Holy Land) having GREAT POWER and the earth (the so-called Negroes) was enlightened with His Glory (wisdom and knowledge of the Truth).

This angel can be no other than Master W. F. Muhammad, the Great Mahdi, who came from the Holy City of Mecca, Arabia, in 1930, and of whom we have spoken before in this book.

The Great Mahdi is indeed the most wise and powerful being on earth (God in Person). It is He who with a strong voice announced the immediate doom of America.

The Great Mahdi said to us that there was no punishment great enough to repay the slavemasters for thier evils against the so-called Negroes of America. He also said that this country is filled with devils and every kind of evil.

His voice was strong and mighty, and to everyone who believed and accepted the True Religion (Islam) he gave a holy name of Allah's. Every word that he said is true. He came for the Salvation of the so-called Negroes, warning them to join on their own kind (the nation of Islam).

America in This Time and Day

All nations are charged with committing

fornication with her (America) and are now angry with her. The merchants of the earth were made rich in trade with her.

America, the richest of all countries, pays the highest wages; she must therefore charge a high price for her merchandise; and those who buy her merchandise for resale must sell for a profit, and they too are thus made rich from such deals.

They shall weep and mourn over her (America), for no man buyeth her merchandise anymore (Rev. 18:11). When people are rich and powerful, they can't see themselves being brought to ought overnight.

Who can remain in power if God has decided against him? "He (Allah) exalts whom He pleases, and whom He pleases He brings to an aught," it says in the Holy Quran.

Nebuchadnezzar and Belshazzar

What does the Bible teach us were the sins of Nebuchadnezzar and Belshazzar that God disgraced and broke up the power of one and outright killed the other (Belshazzar)? Was it not for those silver and golden vessels that were the property of the Temple of God?

It is the Temple's property now (the so-called Negroes) that God is after today. Nebuchadnezzar was charged with bringing them (the silver and golden vessels) from their Temple of God; so is England today charged with bringing into America the first black people to be sold into slavery.

England's Power Will Dwindle

England has lost and still is losing her power over the world of black mankind. Her power will continue to dwindle, until she is left a mere stump of her power in what is called the British Isles.

So-Called Negroes are Sacred in the Eyes of Allah

America has poured wine into those sacred vessels of the Temple of God (the so-called Negroes). Let no man fool you concernig yourselves, my people. You are sacred in the eyes of Allah (God) today.

The so-called Negroes will have to be chastised into the knowledge of Allah, the God of their Salvation.

FEAR NO MORE, my people, for God is on your side today.

Muslims in U. S. Prisons

I receive many letters from inmates of jails and correctional institutions across the country. They are from so-called Negroes who want to accept Islam.

For their benefit I write here that they should send us their slave names and we shall add these to those of other Muslims registered with our Temples of Islam. Later on, as soon as they are free, they should report to the nearest Temple of Islam in person and formally join on to their own Holy Nation of Islam.

Anyone who desires to accept Islam, however, must pledge to serve and obey Allah and His Apostle.

No Muslim Shall Speak Ill of Another

I am not surprised at what the disbelievers (devils) think and say of me. However, when a supposed Brother Muslim joins the disbelievers in (differing from and criticizing) what I write, then I am surely surprised. No Muslim should speak ill of another, especially when they lack correct information about the one they speak of. I know that no TRUE MUSLIM *does* or *will* speak against another to delight the disbelieving people.

If you door today is open to all peoples, which include human devils whom Allah is angry with and whom He threatens with total destruction, I leave it over Him (Allah) to judge between you and me.

Over One Billion Muslims

The true believers of Islam equal in number that of the total population of the whites on our planet (400,000,000). However, by nature *all* members of the black nation are Muslims (lovers of peace), and thus they number well over the one billion mark.

The Glorious Holy Quran Sharrieff

The book that the so-called American Negroes (Tribe of Shabazz) should own and read, the book that the slavemasters have but have not represented it to their slaves, is a book that will heal their sin-sick souls that were made sick and sorrowful by the slavemasters.

This book will open their blinded eyes and open their deaf ears. It will purify them.

A page from the Arabic-language Holy Quran.

The name of this book, which makes a distinction between the God of righteous and the God of evil, is: Glorious Holy Quran Sharrieff. It is indeed the Book of Guidance, of Light and Truth, and of Wisdom and Judgement.

But the average one should first be taught how to respect such a book, how to understand it, and how to teach it. The

Holy Quran Sharrieff contains some of the most beautiful prayers that one has ever heard recited or read. It is called the Glorious Quran and without mistake that is just what it is.

This book, the Holy Quran Sharrieff, is not from a prophet but direct from Allah to Muhammad (may peace and the blessings of Allah be upon him!) not by an angel but from the mouth of Allah (God). And Allah is the Great DISTINGUISH-ER between Truth and falsehood in the judgement of the world, of whom the enemy of truth has ruled the nation of black mankind with falsehood for the past six thousand years.

This book, the Holy Quran Sharrieff, pulls the cover off the covered and shows the nation for the first time that which deceived 90 per cent of the people of the earth without the knowledge of the deceiver.

The Revelation of the Book is from Allah, the Mighty, the Knowing One. And the Book (Holy Quran Sharrieff) is indeed a Guide unto the righteous because the All-Knowing-One and Best Knower has revealed it; and who knows better than Him as to what is best for every living thing?

Man makes himself a fool to try attacking Him (Allah) in arguments. So we have no doubt the Holy Quran Sharrieff is from Allah, the Lord of the worlds. It is one of the clearest-reading books you have ever read.

The God that revealed the Holy Quran Sharrieff to Muhammad (may the peace and blessings of Allah be upon him!) is the same that revealed the scriptures to the other prophets, according to the Holy Quran, which says, "Surely we have revealed to you as we revealed to Noah and the prophets after him; and we revealed to Abraham, Ishmael, Isaac, Jacob, the Tribes, Jesus, Job, Jonah, Aaron, and Solomon; and we gave to David a scripture; and to Moses Allah addressed His words speaking to Him; and we sent Apostles we have mentioned to you before, and Apostles we have not mentioned to you." (4:163, 164)

The Holy Quran's readings are not the kind that will lull one to sleep, but to get a real Holy Quran one should know the Arabic language in which it is written. As for translations, you can find a good one of it by Maulana Muhammad Ali and one by Allama Yusuf Ali.

"That's the honorable Mr. Elijah Mu-hammad!" says little Sister Brenda X., of Philadelphia, pointing to a picture of the Moslem leader which appeared in a recent number of MOSLEM WORLD & THE U. S. A. Holding the magazine is Sister Elizabeth, leader of the Sisters' class in the Philadelphia Temple of Islam. Looking on are Sisters Eleanor X., and Brothers Saladin, Alexander X., David X. and Albert X.

They Bear Witness . . .

By "they," of course, we mean the followers of Mr. Elijah Muhammad, members of the Lost-Found Nation of Islam in America who have accepted Islam and registered their names in the Nation's "Book of Life."

They bear witness that the teachings included in this book are "100 per cent" true and constitute the *only* Solution to the so-called Negroes'-Problem.

There are hundreds of followers of Mr. Elijah Muhammad in the United States who will "do anything—even give our lives" to prove that their leader and teacher is the only man in North America today who can help them in ways in which it is needed.

"Where can I find Mr. Muhammad's followers if I should want to see and talk to them?"—It's not difficult to "find" or recognize

"Mr. Muhammad Speaks"

Each year on February 26, several thousand followers of Mr. Elijah Muhammad assemble in Chicago to pay their respects to the Moslem leader and to have the privilege of meeting him. Our photograph shows Mr. Muhammad addressing the last year's gathering.

53

Ministers trained by Mr. Elijah Muhammad head the various Temples of Islam around the country. Some of them are seen in this photograph which was taken at a recent Atlanta. Ga. Temple of Islam get-together.

them, by *name* or even by *appearance*: they use no surnames (which they have dropped because "they were from the slavemasters") and in appearance they are the nicest gentlemen and ladies you will ever meet among the so-called Negroes of America. (Between themselves the followers of Mr. Elijah Muhammad are known as the "originals.") And you can meet them not only at a Temple of Islam

(perhaps there is one near you) but also at the Temple's various business places, such as restaurants and grocery stores.

Some of the followers of Mr. Elijah Muhammad run their own businesses, in which case you may call on them at their business addresses. They will be happy to meet you, and if you are not a Muslim, you can ask them any questions

54

Chicago's Temple No. 2 grocery, like other Temple enterprises in that city and elsewhere, is known locally as "one of the clednest anywhere."

about Islam that your heart desires.

Each follower of Mr. Elijah Muhammad is a living tribute to the greatness of the Muslim leader, and each business establishment owned by a Temple of Islam or by a Temple member is a proof of Mr. Elijah Muhammad's claim that "IT CAN BE DONE!"—if you know what that means!

The families of Muslims who follow Mr. Elijah Muhammad are happy and devoted families; their homes are abodes of true comfort and peace. Their children have the best manners. They are taught to be righteous and to respect their elders. They NEVER become "juvenile delinquents." All praise is due to Allah!

Many of the followers of Islam under the leadership of Mr. Elijah Muhammad were formerly " absolutely deaf, dumb and blind," for they knew not of self and kind. Today, however, thanks to his Message, they are an awakened and alert people and enjoying a NEW LIFE that is truly the Heaven on Earth.

You too, my lost brothers and sisters, will do well to listen and grasp the Message of Islam as presented by Messenger Muhammad

The University of Islam in Chicago takes care of all the educational and recreational needs of local Muslim children. Mr. Elijah Muhammad plans a similar school in every city where there are sufficient number of Muslims.

and to join on to your own Nation   *day!*
of Righteousness.

Write to your Divine Leader to-

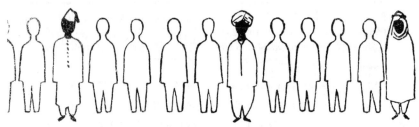

Approximately one out of every four human beings in the world today professes the faith of Islam.